Sonder

poems by

Issa M. Lewis

Finishing Line Press
Georgetown, Kentucky

Sonder

ACKNOWLEDGMENTS

"A ghost is an anchor: a silvered breath" first appeared in *Tule Review* as
"Drown," 2014.

"Never mind who you were—" first appeared in *Blue Lyra Review* as
"Catacomb Saints," 2015.

"One cannot argue with the decisiveness" first appeared in *Rust+Moth* as
"Hanged Man, 1913," 2021.

"You carried a cello as a pack" first appeared in *Gold Wake Live* as "Boy with
Cello," 2020.

"The distance in your eyes speaks" first appeared in *Pink Panther Magazine*
as "Migrant Mother," 2018.

"you didn't need to write it—" first appeared in *Tule Review* as "War Is Hell,"
2014.

"The metal framework behind you" first appeared in *A Quiet Courage* as
"Falling Man," 2015.

"How long you sat, gazing westward" first appeared in *Manzano Mountain
Review* as "Pulling Pieces," 2018.

"Sometimes we can plunge our hands into the earth" first appeared in
Thimble as "Each Pebble," 2021.

"About the size of a bar of soap" first appeared in *CALYX* as "Child's Pose,"
2017, and was runner-up for the 2017 Lois Cranston Memorial Poetry
Prize.

Publisher: Leah Huete de Maines
Editor: Christen Kincaid
Cover Art: Photo by Photoholgic on Unsplash
Author Photo: Photo by Nicole Baker
Cover Design: Elizabeth Maines McCleavy

Order online: www.finishinglinepress.com
also available on amazon.com

Author inquiries and mail orders:
Finishing Line Press
PO Box 1626
Georgetown, Kentucky 40324
USA

Index of First Lines

Sonder
n. the realization that each random passerby is living a life as vivid and complex as your own

I.

Inside every eye is yet another curve
reversed, reflecting, another image
projected. If we look closely enough
we can see it. We realize
their face is our face, their feet
our feet. What sweetness
to see their wanderings.

II.

A ghost is an anchor: a silvered breath
of what came before, a bookmark.

Look for them among crumbling stones
and rotting wood; search for orbs

or streaks of light. Inhale deeply
half-formed mists like cold night air

biting the lungs. The years have sharp teeth.
The search for ghosts keeps us tethered,

unable to abandon what we loved before.
Grasp them with too much longing, and drown.

III.

There are so few times
when I am so mindful
of where I step.
Every footfall might
put me in a position
of disrespect,
my sole to someone's soul,
or their bones. I wonder
do their souls linger?
Would they stay here
with their bones,
their stones?

IV.

We think of stone as time,
a defiant shape. Its face
gazes at the sky, impassive,
a challenge. We see it unmoving,
though we are moved by all
the years it contains. We put
words on stone, graven or relief,
because we want to remember—
the sky eats memories.

V.

After the "catacomb saints," Christian martyrs made into relics
by the Catholic Church

Never mind who you were—
you may have worn rags soiled with sweat
and blood. Maybe they barely covered
your body and you tugged the unfinished hems
up or down to salvage your dignity
as you were dragged through the tunnel.
The archway ahead of you roared light
so you closed your eyes and whispered
Jesus.

When you awoke, you were bones
and gold. Heaven was darker than you thought
it would be, full of echoes of dripping water.
Strings of light crept in from cracks above
like golden ribbons keeping your skeleton intact.
Every piece of you glittered and clinked,
rings on every finger. You held chalices and swords,
an underground king ruling over rats.

Who you are now is faded and brittle
as old paper. The sapphires in your eyes dulled
a hundred years ago, when people stopped looking
beyond the bones, when they could no longer imagine
your face not encrusted with gold.

VI.

Genus. n. A Class of things that have common characteristics

At our roots we have *spread*, we have *soil*, we have feet germinating, toes scrabbling below. Above are nascent beings, squinting in the sun. We have *awareness*, we have *disorientation*, we have *longing* for progeniture because the upward pathvis unknown. We have *faces*, we have *difference*, we have *distrust* and *malignance* because we have lost sight of our innate similarities, that place where our feet tangle and touch in the grit. Our cognates. We have *familiar*, we have *same*, but we have forgotten that.

VII.

One cannot argue with the decisiveness
of a wooden beam. The fact of a roof slant.
Hard edges speak to finality, to a choice
firmly made. In Ryder-Waite, the hanged man
is head-down, suspended by a single foot,
The other leg crosses behind, a casual dangle.
It may be interpreted as *surrender* or *sacrifice*
or *breaking old patterns.* I see
a straight line between a painful present
and an ecstatic oblivion.
Another interpretation is *suspended in time*
and that's what you became: a nameless man
cut from a rafter and laid in the ground
with no ceremony, no stone, nothing
to remember you but a scant entry
etched in a ledger: *unknown male,
hanged himself, 11/4/1913.* This
is your conclusion, to obscure yourself
in rest. A hundred years later,
I only know where you are, never
who you were. *Old patterns broken,
a missed opportunity.*

VIII.

A name is a constellation, guiding us
through our minutiae. Look up—
the star-steps scatter
into so many pathways
that could be chosen,
but which one leads
to a long life? The tiny stones
have lambs, or rose buds,
but no names. They peek
out of the grass, little breadcrumbs,
a trail back to a mother's empty arms.

IX.

You grew out voluptuous and inappropriate,
conjured from blood and breath
and landed on a strange shore.
And when you had filled your vessel,
licked every drop of sustenance from the walls,
you curled, let your blood grow sluggish and dark
and sighed yourself into a granite sleep.
Layer after layer settled and smoothed
your features clean. On the outside,
your mother's hand curved over roundness
that no longer had place, as if she could
polish your skin into golden pearl.

X.

*After the photo of unnamed Romany boy, taken by
Eva Besnyö, 1931*

You carried a cello as a pack,
so much bigger than ragtag you.
The weight of the ravaged world on your back,

so young to understand hunger and lack.
So small, but you knew what you had to do.
You carried a cello as a pack

and wandered tree-lined cul-de-sacs
in your brother's worn-out leather shoes.
The weight of the ravaged world on your back

as wood, as heavy air reverberating back
against the bow, as the coins bystanders carelessly threw.
You carried a cello as a pack

but no one carried you, even as your limbs went slack
with exhaustion, with the sheer weight of what you knew.
The weight of the ravaged world on your back,

little Roma, busking between war clouds gathering black.
No one stayed or listened long to find out if you grew.
You carried a cello as a pack,
the weight of the ravaged world on your back.

XI.

After the "Migrant Mother" photo of Florence Owens Thompson,
taken by Dorothea Lange, 1936

The distance in your eyes speaks
of the dullness of hunger. You are all
sharp edges and angles, though you make
softness in your arms for your infant:
a mother's skill to make nourishment
from nothing.

Hands that some days scrape themselves raw
pulling cotton, or vegetables from their beds,
hold tight to the child in your lap, to skin
that hasn't yet known work, still smooth cream.

Your story stays tucked in your tent.
Everyone thinks sun darkened your skin,
and that your poverty is some other color.

XII.

"She did the best she could." –Engraved on the headstone of Emma Weldon, 1859-1936

Long ago there was a woman
whom I will never know
who raised some children
and committed some sins
and made dinners for families
who lost loved ones
and argued with her husband
sometimes and slammed a door
when she was angry
and taught her daughters
how to sew and make soup
and buried a three-year-old son
and accepted dinners after
from the neighbors she'd fed before.
And now here, on this stone
bearing her name, all I can know
is when she came into this world
and when she left it
and that some well-meaning relative
shrugged their shoulders
for an epitaph
and left it at that.

XIII.

*After the "War Is Hell" photo of Vietnam War soldier
Larry Wayne Chaffin, taken by Horst Faas, 1965*

you didn't need to write it—
the faded fabric on your helmet tells the story
of a thousand razor suns

your upturned eyes are not cups of self-pity
but the quirked corner of your mouth
says *I can't un-see, not even myself*

the photographer didn't take down your name—
he snapped his flash and burned your skin
into the landscape of his film

in the negatives, your pupils must glow
like napalm

XIV.

For Andy Horujko, who walked from Anchorage, Alaska to Tierra del Fuego, 1970-1972

I hope you will forgive us for creeping into your home, Andy. The door was propped open by echoes and dust motes and the wide gray sky had its watch on us—we had to. Your stone in the nearby cemetery was neatly tended by your neighbors who remembered you to us. As though memory could transport you to another place. It wasn't memory that took you from Anchorage to Tierra del Fuego—it was feet and feeling and homemade shoes, after a while. But maybe memory did bring you home again to this tiny cabin made of wood you split yourself. We needed to see what was left of a life spent putting one foot in front of the other, needed to know what you'd make of this stony sky in August.

XV.

After the photo of the unnamed "tank man" protester in
Tiananmen Square, taken by Jeff Widener, 1989

That morning, you woke up. You showered,
put on pants. There were angry voices echoing outside
as they had for days like a weary loop, but you needed groceries
so you left your home and walked—how many blocks?—
let's say three—to a corner store.

The first time you looked both ways, there was nothing.
But while you were at the store, the air turned solid with sound.
The cashier held his ears and you clung to your purchases
as the counter trembled. Maybe the eggs fell,
their yellow insides seeping into the grooves of the tile floor.

Filling your bags, you made your way back to the street.
This time, you looked up as the concrete before you crumbled
under the weight of caterpillar treads, a cannon's dark eye trained
on you.

A weightless moment—breath, a whiff of hot metal and diesel—
a decision. The emphatic choice to stand, bags full
of mundane, human necessities and maybe even a candy bar
purchased on a whim—

to stand, chocolate melting in the June sun, bringing the world
into stillness.

XVI.

After the "Falling Man" photo of the September 11, 2011
terrorist attacks, taken by Richard Drew

The metal framework behind you
is gone now; it followed you down
that day, exhausted by the effort
of staying upright, of breathing smoke.
You heard someone scream *oh shit, oh shit—*

but you whispered to the horrified eyes
watching your body tumble into
a headfirst decision: *it's okay*
once you get used to feel of it

Below, a nest of girders and concrete
for you to rest in. The wing of an airplane
shaded your dimming eyes. Then there was silence.

it's okay you whispered

the fall will last your lifetime

XVII.

The last remaining house on Holland Island in Chesapeake Bay, MD, built in 1888, collapsed in 2010 due to the island's erosion

How long you sat, gazing westward,
your glassy eyes reflecting the sunset,
sighing at high tide. Who would have thought
the ocean could be thirsty, could lap
at soft shores of mud and silt
until they melted away. Pulling pieces,
one board at a time, a nail rusted, a headstone
smoothed and bleached, toppled over;
each window a gasping breath.

Fishermen lived here, built their boats here,
gathered shad and oysters here until
the ocean encroached: each lick of wave
erasing their footprints as the shoreline gave way.
You saw children born in your rooms,
felt their feet patter on your wooden floors.
You held their grief when elders passed,
carried it once everyone had gone.

One by one, your fellows buckled, shuffled off
into that mouth filled with fish and brine.
sliding into water and floating away,
a funeral no one heard. You stood on high ground,
sea birds taking refuge in your attic,
so much longer than anyone ever stood
on that island.

In the flotsam a final breath:
collapse, relief, stretched
in all directions. Those walls
could no sooner hold up the sky
than contain those years alone.

XVIII.

For the Sperl family, 3/29/21

Sometimes we can plunge our hands into the earth
and find crystals. Other times just rocks,
blunt objects upon which we must write
our own meaning. This was a day of rocks,
when you changed direction with dizzying speed,
grounded then airborne, with us then not in a flip:

we had to write meaning on that, too. How we wanted
to throw those rocks at the sky. Ugly, dumb rocks
with no shimmer or glint. Gray as the ash of burned grass,
of wet asphalt, of a too-long night. Blunt as bad news
over the phone.

We kept digging in the earth for something
we wanted to keep, stared at our dusty hands and looked
for meaning, for how to live in a world
that doesn't sparkle anymore. We cast the gravel we found
like mystics, divining. Each pebble
tried to tell us something,

but we don't speak the language of stones.

XIX.

*After the photo of the September 2, 2015 death of 3- year old
Alan Kurdi, taken by Nilüfer Demir*

About the size of a bar of soap,
and equally waterlogged. What tiny
pieces of leather these are, neatly
side by side. *Child's pose,* it's called,
little rump in the air, hands reaching behind,
cheek to the ground like a young one sleeps
at night. Alan, do you dream
as the sand embraces you more
with each wave's lap? A gentle nest
of apologies.

No home, behind the boat or in front,
so the water claimed you—it meant to be
peaceful, like a mother's hand
leading you across a parking lot
to a safer place, where no metal screamed
or bit into anyone, where your surname
could be something other than *Kurdi,*
other than *Other.* Alan, do you dream
of naming every grain of sand
yourself, touching them with your pudgy
toddler fingertips, letting them
swirl in your palm, cupped in a puddle of ocean?
Snuggle into your nest and consider
the vastness of unnamed waters,
your smallness within it.

There will be hands on you, Alan,
pulling you from the water. They will be
exceedingly gentle. They will wipe the sand
from your belly, your cheek; they will
replace your soaked clothes with dry.
It will feel as though you are being born
a second time, lifting you from the mellow
rocking you called home for a short while,

and there will be tears. Someone
will stroke your hair like your mother did,
arranging it into a soft forehead curl
once it dries. Darling Alan, do you dream
of whose hands will reach for you
as you leave this brackish, littered place
and drift away?

XX.

Most only see stones. Names and dates and nothing more. I see pieces of a quilt stitched together in the grass, scrappy bits of lives I never got to see but recognize as my own. I want to whisper to them and have my voice trickle down through the dirt: *I will be the thread.*

Issa M. Lewis is the author of *Infinite Collisions* (Finishing Line Press, 2017) and *Anchor* (Kelsay Books, 2022). She is the 2013 recipient of the Lucille Clifton Poetry Prize and a runner-up for the 2017 Lois Cranston Memorial Poetry Prize. In 2019, she served as the inaugural Artist-in-Residence for the Mackinac State Historic Parks program on Mackinac Island. Her poems have previously appeared or are forthcoming in *Rust+Moth, Thimble, North American Review, South Carolina Review, The Banyan Review,* and *Panoply*, amongst others, and her book reviews have recently appeared in *The Banyan Review* and *Split Rock Review.* She lives in West Michigan with her family and teaches English and Communications at Davenport University.

www.ingramcontent.com/pod-product-compliance
Lightning Source LLC
Chambersburg PA
CBHW022107080426
42734CB00009B/1508